Let's Danc

Irish Step Dancing

By Mark Thomas

Children's Press
A Division of Grolier Publishing
New York / London / Hong Kong / Sydney
Danbury, Connecticut

Thanks to the students of the Cara School of Irish Dance

Photo Credits: Cover and all photos by Maura Boruchow
Contributing Editor: Jeri Cipriano
Book Design: Michael DeLisio

Visit Children's Press on the Internet at:
http://publishing.grolier.com

Library of Congress Cataloging-in-Publication Data

Thomas, Mark, 1963-
  Irish step dancing / by Mark Thomas.
    p. cm. — (Let's dance)
  Includes bibliographical references and index.
  ISBN 0-516-23143-X (lib. bdg.)—ISBN 0-516-23068-9 (pbk.)
  1. Step dancing—Juvenile literature. [1. Step dancing.] I. Title.

GV1793 .T56 2000
793.3—dc21

                                             00-043185

Contents

1 Meet Rosa 4

2 Soft-Shoe Dances 6

3 Dancing in a Show 18

4 New Words 22

5 To Find Out More 23

6 Index 24

7 About the Author 24

My name is Rosa.

I am learning Irish
step dancing.

5

I wear soft shoes to dance.

7

Irish step dancing is danced to Irish music.

I move my feet to the music.

I keep my arms at my sides.

I learn Irish step dancing in a class.

My friends are dancers, too.

Our teacher shows us **dance steps.**

This dance step is the **reel**.

It is a fast dance step.

13

Another dance step is the **light jig**.

This step is not as fast as the reel.

15

We put on a show after we learn our dance steps.

We dance on a **stage**.

We wear costumes in the show.

We dance in a line.

ST. EUGENE

19

We dance well during the show.

We always take a **bow** after the show.

New Words

bow (**bahw**) bending from
the waist

dance steps (**dans stepz**) ways to
move your feet while dancing

light jig (**lyt jig**) a slow dance step

reel (**reel**) a fast dance step

stage (**stayg**) an area above the
floor where shows are put on

To Find Out More

Books
Irish Dance
by Arthur Flynn and Anne Farrall
Pelican Publishing

Irish Dancing
by Tom Quinn
Collins Celtic

Web Site
Virtual Ireland
http://www.virtualireland.com
This site contains a lot of information about Ireland.

Index

bow, 20

costumes, 18

dance steps, 10, 16

light jig, 14

reel, 12, 14

stage, 16

About the Author

Mark Thomas is a writer and educator who lives in Florida.

Reading Consultants

Kris Flynn, Coordinator, Small School District Literacy, The San Diego County Office of Education

Shelly Forys, Certified Reading Recovery Specialist, W.J. Zahnow Elementary School, Waterloo, IL

Peggy McNamara, Professor, Bank Street College of Education, Reading and Literacy Program